REGINA
VA

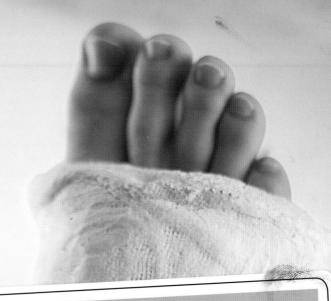

POWERFUL MEDICINE

# SHATTERED BONES
## TRUE SURVIVAL STORIES

### SANDRA MARKLE

LERNER PUBLICATIONS COMPANY · MINNEAPOLIS

**NOTE FROM THE AUTHOR**

The books in the Powerful Medicine series are the result of long, exciting detective work that let me talk to amazing, caring physicians, surgeons, and researchers. I also got to know patients who faced some of the worst moments of their lives with determination and courage. I consider all of the people you'll meet in the Powerful Medicine series heroes—their stories are truly remarkable. You'll also discover, as I did, how wonderful the human body really is.

## FOR CURIOUS KIDS EVERYWHERE—THEY'RE THE FUTURE!

ACKNOWLEDGMENTS: The author would like to thank the following people for taking the time to share their expertise: Dr. Mauro Ferrari, University of Texas Health Science Center, Houston; Dr. Paul Reiman, orthopedic surgeon, Temecula, California; Dr. Franklin Shuler, Vanderbilt University Hospital; Dr. Russell Stewart, University of California, Santa Barbara; Dr. John Stith, Cardinal Glennon Children's Hospital, Saint Louis, Missouri; Dr. Joyce Tarbet, Chicago orthopedic surgeon for the U.S. Women's Soccer Team; Dr. Jonathan Pascoe, Ilam Medical Centre, Christchurch, New Zealand; and Dr. James Urbaniak, Duke University.

A special thank-you to Skip Jeffery for his loving support during the creative process

Lerner Publications Company
A division of Lerner Publishing Group, Inc.
241 First Avenue North
Minneapolis, MN 55401 U.S.A.

Website address: www.lernerbooks.com


Library of Congress Cataloging-in-Publication Data

Markle, Sandra.
    Shattered bones: true survival stories / by Sandra Markle.
        p.    cm. — (Powerful medicine)
  Includes bibliographical references and index.
  ISBN 978–0–8225–8703–3 (lib. bdg. : alk. paper)
    1. Bones—Juvenile literature. 2. Bones—Wounds and injuries—Juvenile literature. I. Title.
  QP88.2.M175  2011
  617.4'71044—dc22                                        2009034442

Manufactured in the United States of America
1 - DP - 7/15/10

# CONTENTS

Most of the time, we don't think about how our bodies keep us healthy and active. But if something happens to one body part, we notice what isn't working as it should. **Our bones are one key body part.** They are the body's sturdy framework. In this book, you will find real-life stories of people whose bones are not just broken. They are badly damaged. The stories also tell of the doctors who work to repair injured bones. They show how science and technology help to make amazing recoveries possible.

# CRASH!

**IT WAS A HOT, SUNNY JUNE DAY IN BALTIMORE,** Maryland, and the Freestyle Motocross (FMX) finals were in full swing. The crowd watched riders doing 360-degree flips, backflips, no-hand landings, and more. One of the stars of

the show was Blake "Bilko" Williams *(right)*. For his trick, he hung suspended from the handlebars of his motorcycle as it made a complete backflip. His performance excited the crowd. The judges were impressed. His trick put him into second place in the games. **But when he tried to repeat the trick during the next round of the finals, it didn't go well.**

Bilko fell. He was so high that it was like jumping off a two-story building. He slammed onto his feet as he landed. Then he collapsed. Several of his friends and the other riders ran onto the track and carried him off. His legs and feet weren't cut or bleeding. But his left foot hurt and was twisted. His right leg hurt too. Clearly something was wrong. He was rushed to the hospital.

The medical team used an X-ray machine to see inside Bilko's feet and legs. An X-ray machine shoots high-energy rays, called X-rays, through the body part being examined. Here the technician places a special plate connected to a computer beneath the broken leg. Wherever X-rays pass through, the area appears light gray on the computer screen. Wherever something solid inside the body blocks the X-rays, dark shapes appear on the screen. The X-ray of Bilko's left foot and ankle and right leg showed a lot of solid shapes. These were his bones. Some were clearly broken. One bone in his left foot was shattered—broken into many small pieces.

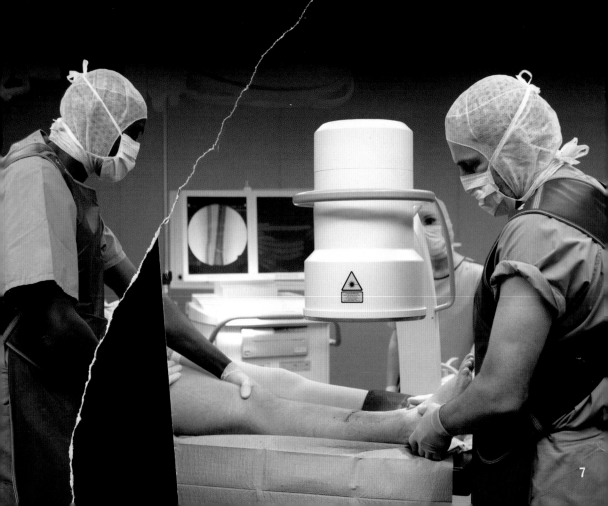

**BONES ARE HARD BODY PARTS. BUT THEY ARE STILL LIVING TISSUE MADE UP OF CELLS, THE BODY'S BUILDING BLOCKS.** Bone tissue forms when special cells, called osteoblasts, make proteins— substances that build body parts—that spread outward in all directions. The proteins crisscross to trap the osteoblasts inside the network. As blood flows through this network, calcium—a kind of mineral—in the blood collects in the network. The calcium hardens it into bone. The trapped osteoblasts become mature bone cells. These are called osteocytes. The job of osteocytes is to control the amount of calcium in the bones and keep them strong.

**Like other living tissues, bone tissue breaks down and is replaced.** Osteoblasts make new bone tissue. At the same time, other special cells, called osteoclasts, dissolve and reabsorb bone minerals. Working together, osteoblasts, osteocytes, and osteoclasts keep bone tissue healthy. They also maintain the bone's structure and its shape.

hard Kessel & Dr. Randy Kardon | Tissues & Organs | Visuals Unlimited, Inc.

Each
with

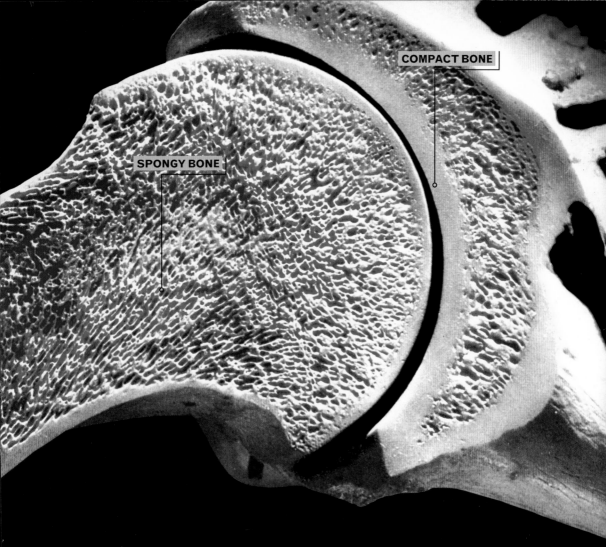

COMPACT BONE

SPONGY BONE

Like a stack of sandwiches, bone cells are arranged between layers of collagen fibers. Collagen is a tough, rubbery material. The layers of bone and collagen may be stacked to form either spongy bone or compact bone. Spongy bone has lots of spaces or cavities. This makes spongy bone lightweight. The cavities aren't empty, though. They're filled with blood vessels, nerves, and bone marrow. Bone marrow is a soft material that contains fat and special cells that produce new blood cells. Compact bone is made up of layers that are tightly packed together. Compact bone contains spaces too. However, these cavities are so small they can only be seen through a microscope. This structure makes compact bone strong and helps it resist shocks.

AS YOU ALREADY DISCOVERED, BONES ARE HARD, BUT THEY ARE NOT SOLID. In addition to the spaces between bone cells, there are canals. Canals are tubelike openings that blood vessels and nerves pass through. Bones also have a central cavity.

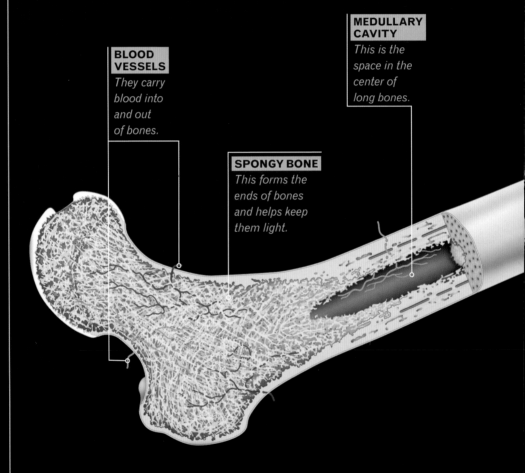

**MEDULLARY CAVITY**
*This is the space in the center of long bones.*

**BLOOD VESSELS**
*They carry blood into and out of bones.*

**SPONGY BONE**
*This forms the ends of bones and helps keep them light.*

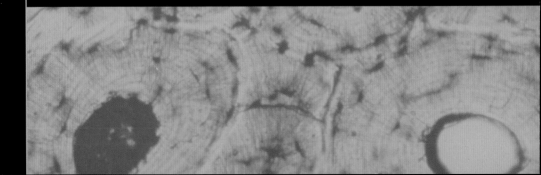

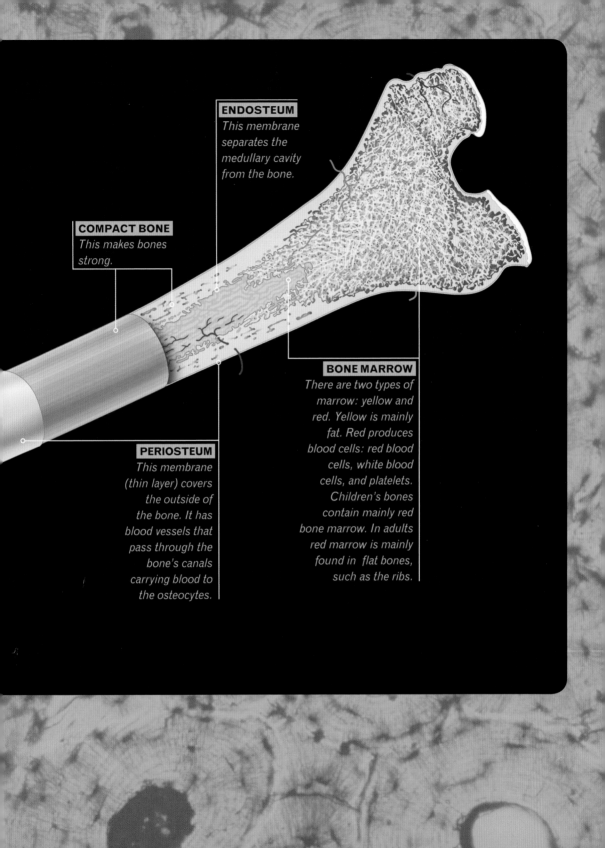

**ENDOSTEUM**
*This membrane separates the medullary cavity from the bone.*

**COMPACT BONE**
*This makes bones strong.*

**BONE MARROW**
*There are two types of marrow: yellow and red. Yellow is mainly fat. Red produces blood cells: red blood cells, white blood cells, and platelets. Children's bones contain mainly red bone marrow. In adults red marrow is mainly found in flat bones, such as the ribs.*

**PERIOSTEUM**
*This membrane (thin layer) covers the outside of the bone. It has blood vessels that pass through the bone's canals carrying blood to the osteocytes.*

All the body's bones work together to create a strong framework—the skeleton. The skeleton gives a body its shape. The skeleton also protects soft organs, such as the heart and lungs. Stretchy bands, called ligaments, hold bones together. Other bands, called tendons, attach muscles to the bones of the skeleton. As muscles contract, they pull on the bones to move them.

Bones can't bend much. So the skeleton has joints, places where the bones meet. Joints let the body bend and move. Feet and hands are made up of lots of small bones. So they have lots of joints. Think of the many different ways feet and hands can bend and move!

Babies are born with 300 bones. Some of them fuse together over time. Because of this, adults have 206 bones.

# THE BODY'S FRAMEWORK

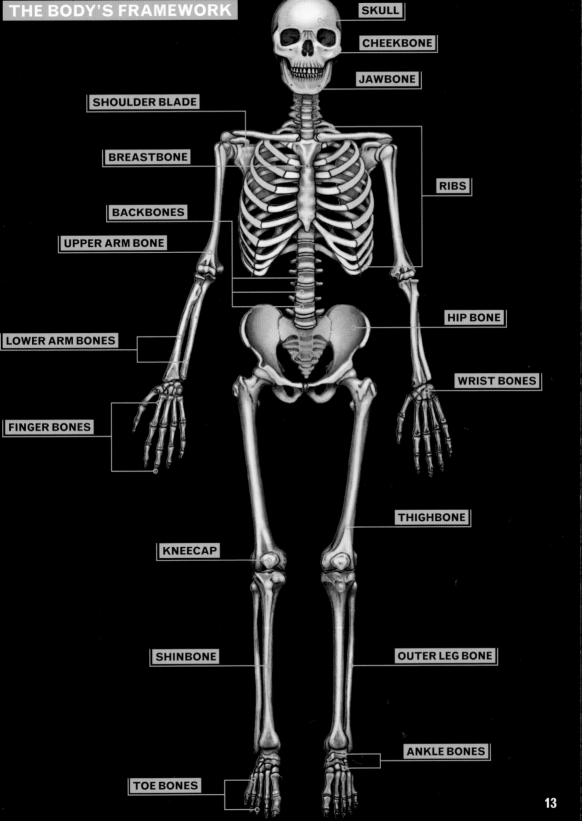

SKULL

CHEEKBONE

JAWBONE

SHOULDER BLADE

BREASTBONE

RIBS

BACKBONES

UPPER ARM BONE

LOWER ARM BONES

HIP BONE

WRIST BONES

FINGER BONES

THIGHBONE

KNEECAP

SHINBONE

OUTER LEG BONE

ANKLE BONES

TOE BONES

# FIXING THE BREAKS

**BECAUSE OF THE WAY BONES ARE MADE, THE HUMAN SKELETON IS LIGHTWEIGHT AND STRONG.** It can withstand shocks. Bones can even bend a little. But when a strong force hits bones, something has to give. The medical team treating Bilko was not surprised to see some of the bones in his left foot were dislocated. This means they were shifted out of their proper places. Other bones in his left foot and right leg were fractured, or broken. One bone in his left foot was shattered or broken into lots of pieces.

**There are two main types of fractures—open and closed.** In an open fracture, a part of a broken bone pokes through the skin. In a closed fracture, the broken pieces are still inside the body. All Bilko's fractures were closed fractures.

Bilko's broken bones were separated from one another along the break. This is called a complete fracture. Some of the broken pieces of the bones in his foot could be put back in line without surgery.

Bilko said, "The doctors gave me something for the pain. Then they pushed and pulled on my foot. I could hear the crunching as they put the fractured ends together again."

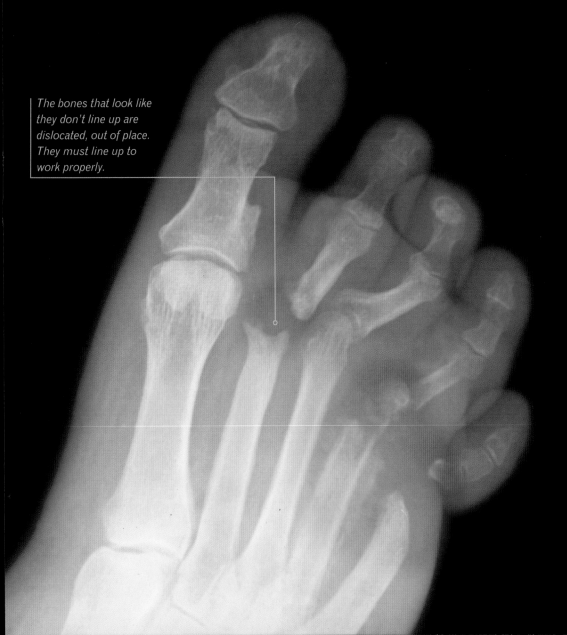

The bones that look like they don't line up are dislocated, out of place. They must line up to work properly.

Next, Bilko had surgery to repair the shattered bone in his left foot. The medical team made an incision (cut) in his foot. They removed all the smallest bits of bone. These had separated from the periosteum, so they had no blood supply carrying nutrients and oxygen to them. Without this, the tiny bones were dead.

Bilko's surgeon, Dr. Paul Reiman, said, "We had to take out all those bits so they wouldn't migrate [travel] to where they didn't belong. They might go to the sole of the foot and be like walking on gravel. Or they might lodge in a nearby joint. That would keep it from moving properly and be painful."

After the team removed the small bits, they lined up the remaining pieces of the bone. Then they stitched up the incision. The team inserted stainless steel pins and a stainless steel screw through the skin. These would hold the broken ends of the bone together while they became whole once more. After they healed, the doctor would remove the pins.

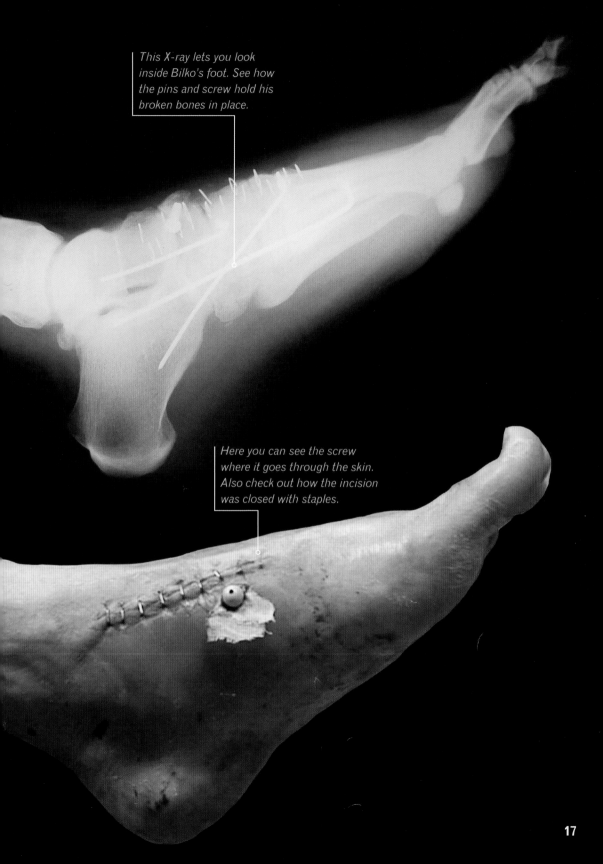

This X-ray lets you look inside Bilko's foot. See how the pins and screw hold his broken bones in place.

Here you can see the screw where it goes through the skin. Also check out how the incision was closed with staples.

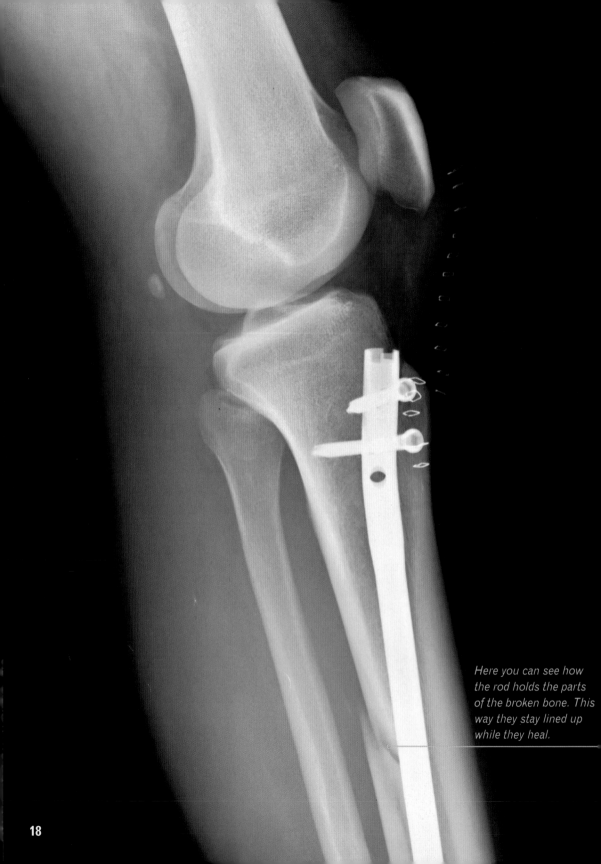

*Here you can see how the rod holds the parts of the broken bone. This way they stay lined up while they heal.*

Next, the medical team went to work on Bilko's broken right leg. They made an incision in it to reach the fractured bone, the shinbone (tibia). After the pieces were lined up, the team used a special surgical instrument to drill straight down through the medullary cavity of the bone pieces. The hole it made was just big enough for the team to slide a long metal rod through it. The rod would keep the pieces lined up while they healed. The rod would be left in Bilko's leg bone forever, so it was made of titanium, a lightweight metal. Titanium also bends slightly under pressure, similar to the way living bone does.

TO FURTHER PROTECT BROKEN BONES WHILE THEY HEAL, THEY MAY BE COVERED BY A SPLINT OR A CAST. A splint is something stiff, such as metal or plastic that's strapped in place around the fracture site. A cast is a hard covering, such as plaster of Paris or fiberglass, that surrounds the broken area. It holds the bone pieces in place while they heal.

**A FRACTURED BONE MAY ALSO BE KEPT STILL WITH A CAGELIKE DEVICE.** This applies pressure where it's needed to keep broken pieces of a bone lined up. Then, like an assembled puzzle, the bone pieces stay in their correct places while the bone heals.

# SAVING ALISHA'S FACE

**ON JULY 27, 2008, ALISHA CAPPS WAS PITCHING FOR HER SOFTBALL TEAM,** the Saint Louis Esprit. It was an important game—the U.S. Under-Eighteen Nationals. Alisha wound up and released the ball. It went high and outside. No one expected the batter to connect, but she did. *Crack!* The ball came flying back at Alisha. She tried to turn away, but she couldn't react fast enough. The softball slammed into her right cheek.

Alisha needed surgery to repair her shattered bones. But screws, pins, and rods weren't the right tools for holding the pieces together. **That's because she shattered the very delicate bones of her face.**

With the championship at stake, Alisha puts her all into the pitch.

Alisha was rushed to the hospital. X-rays showed that the bones forming her cheek and surrounding her eye were shattered.

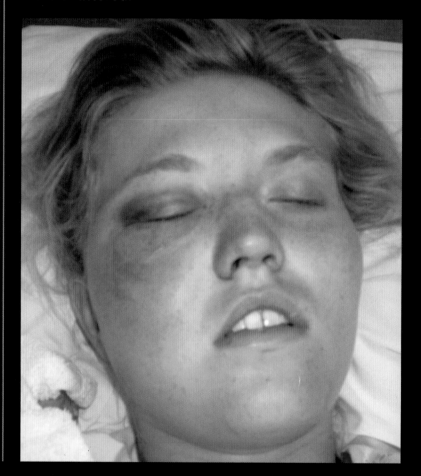

The X-rays showed that the bones that form the roof of her mouth were broken too. So were her upper and lower jawbones.

Luckily, Alisha's teeth were okay. However, the broken jawbones meant the teeth were not lined up properly.

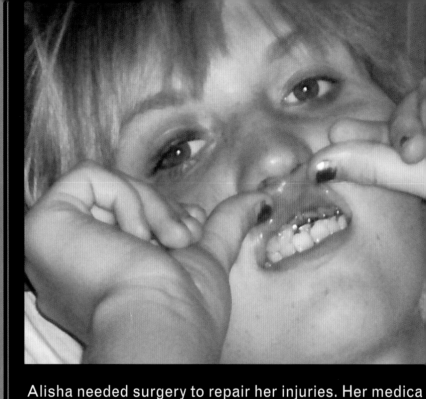

Alisha needed surgery to repair her injuries. Her medical
team screwed a metal bar through her gums into her
upper jawbone. Her teeth were wired to this bar. The
broken parts of her jawbone were wired together too.
While these bones healed, the only way Alisha could eat
was to suck liquids through a straw.

Alisha's shattered facial bones had to be supported while they healed. Her surgeon, Dr. John Stith, inserted pieces of titanium wire mesh to form the shape of her cheekbones. He carefully moved the bone bits and placed them, one at a time, on the titanium mesh. As he worked, he made sure the bone bits stayed attached to their soft tissue and blood supply.

Dr. Stith said, "One thing that helps when facial bones break is that the blood supply to that area is especially good. So even shattered bones tend to heal very, very well."

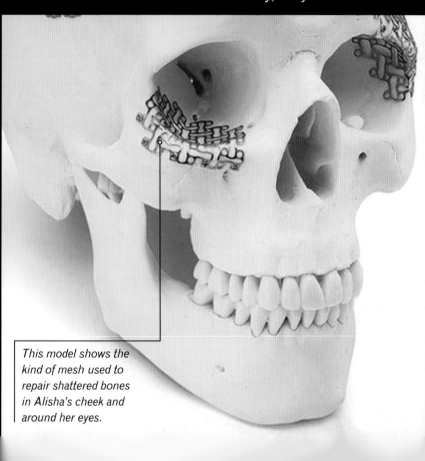

This model shows the kind of mesh used to repair shattered bones in Alisha's cheek and around her eyes.

# HEALING

**WHEN BONES BREAK,** the healing process starts immediately. **The body releases chemicals at the injury site that increase blood flow to that area.** This makes the fracture site swell. The chemicals also signal the blood to send extra white blood cells to the site. These cells attack invading germ cells, which could cause an infection. They also remove dead tissue cells.

Bilko hated not being able to ride. Just getting around was a struggle. He had to keep his weight off his leg while the broken bones healed.

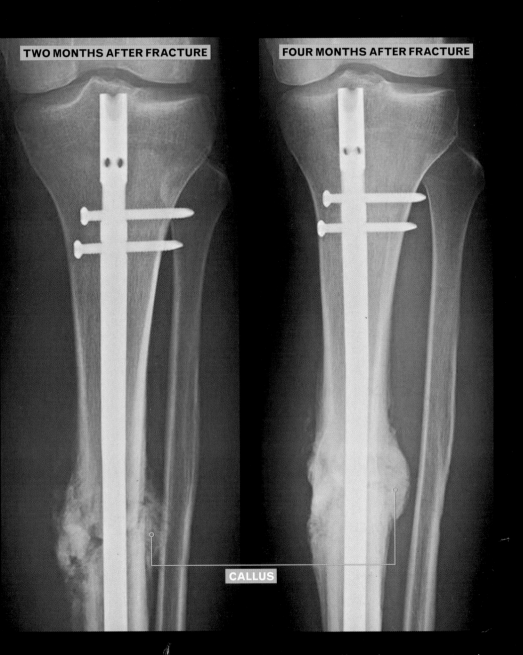

CALLUS

Osteoblasts, the bone-tissue-forming cells, also move to the fracture site. Gradually, a collar of bone tissue, called a callus, builds up around the break. The callus reconnects the bone pieces on either side of the fracture. Blood vessels from the surrounding tissue enter this new bone tissue. They carry oxygen and food nutrients.

Slowly the fracture fills in with tissue. At first, this tissue is rubbery. Then calcium from the blood moves into the tissue, and it becomes hard. Because children have a thicker periosteum than adults, their bone tissue has a better blood supply. That helps a child's bones heal faster than an adult's. Sometimes a child's bones heal in as little as three to six weeks. A healthy adult's bones usually take about eight weeks to heal. Bilko's took even longer. He developed an infection in his left foot, and he had to return to the hospital. In the hospital, he received a strong antibiotic to fight the infection. Then his bones, especially his shattered bone, could heal.

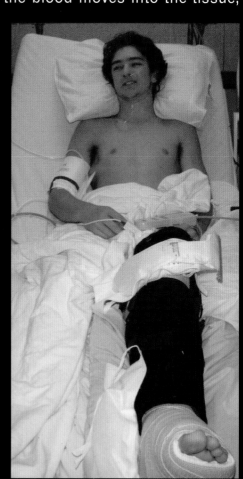

Finally, Bilko's bones
were strong enough
for him to start riding
again.

WHEN A CHILD BREAKS A BONE, ESPECIALLY A LEG OR AN ARM BONE, HE OR SHE FACES AN ADDED RISK. The growth plate is a special disk near the end of these bones. A break could separate the disk from the bone's shaft. This disk needs to be attached to the shaft for the bone to grow longer. Cells that form on the shaft side of the plate produce more cells. Like adding onto a stack of paper cups, these cells lengthen the bone. As the bone grows longer, the child grows taller.

DR. REIMAN SAID, "IF THE GROWTH PLATE IS SEPARATED FROM THE REST OF THE BONE, WE HAVE TO RECONNECT IT. And we have to line it up exactly where it was connected before for bone growth to continue normally. We can do that because, usually, the growth plate isn't a straight line. It's a wavy line. And we line up the waves. If we do that, we have a fighting chance the growth plate will continue to function. Then the bone's growth will continue until it just naturally stops. That usually happens when girls are in their late teens and boys are in their early twenties."

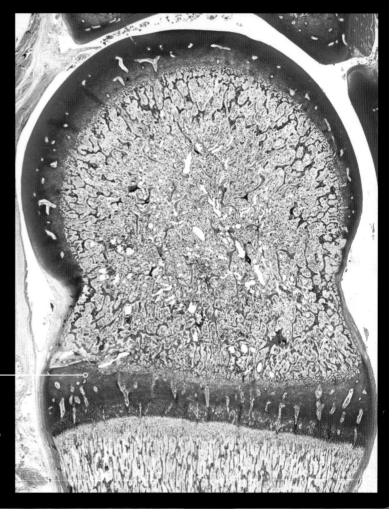

**GROWTH PLATE**
*Here you can see the growth plate near the head of the femur, the thighbone.*

# BONE HELPERS

**JACK GRIFFETH DIDN'T HAVE AN ACCIDENT THAT DAMAGED HIS BONES.** His bones were damaged because he was given chemotherapy, big doses of strong drugs, to treat his cancer. The drugs cured his cancer, but they had a serious side effect. They caused a decreased blood supply to the heads of his femurs, his thighbones. **As a result, some of the bone tissue in that area died.** Jack said, "I loved hiking, biking, skiing—all kinds of outdoor activities. But walking and even standing became very painful."

The head of the thighbone forms an important part of the hip joint. This joint is made up of the head of the femur and a cup-shaped pocket in the pelvis, the hip bone. Normally, the head of each femur is round and any movement of the leg makes it slide smoothly inside the hip bone pocket. Because some of the bone tissue died in the heads of Jack's femurs, they became irregular in shape. Any movement of his hip joints was jerky and painful.

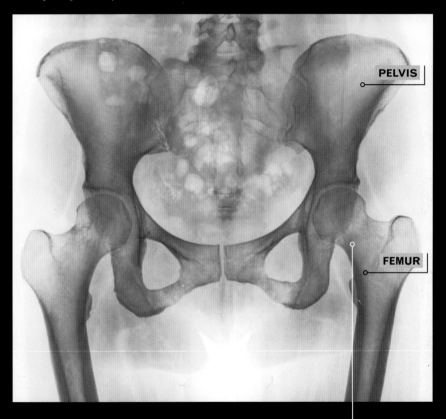

PELVIS

FEMUR

*The head of the femur is attached to the long shaft by a thin neck. When the joint doesn't work normally, the femur is at risk of breaking at this point.*

If they had been left untreated, the heads of his femurs could someday collapse. One way of fixing faulty hip joints, like Jack's, is with an artificial ball-and-socket joint. Surgeons cut away the damaged head of the femur. Then they insert a replacement metal head into the remaining bone.

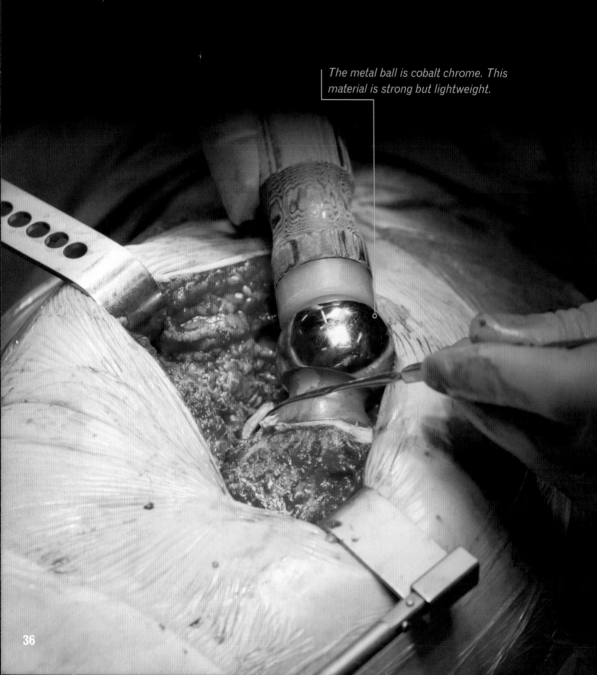

The metal ball is cobalt chrome. This material is strong but lightweight.

A plastic cup is inserted into the hip bone. Then the metal head can move freely inside this cup. This artificial joint works well, but not as well as a real joint. Jack wanted to continue to do all the things he loved doing. He even wanted to continue climbing mountains. He wanted hip joints that worked normally.

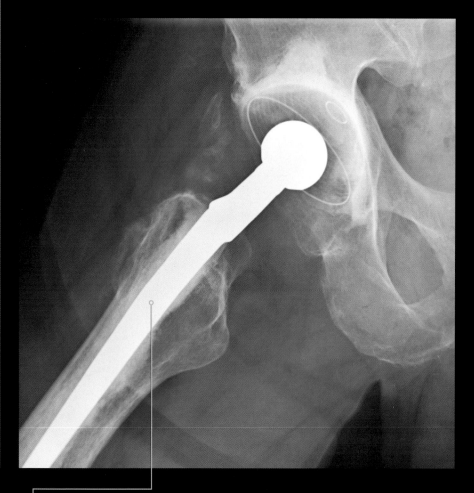

This X-ray lets you look inside the body and see how the artificial ball and socket joint fit together.

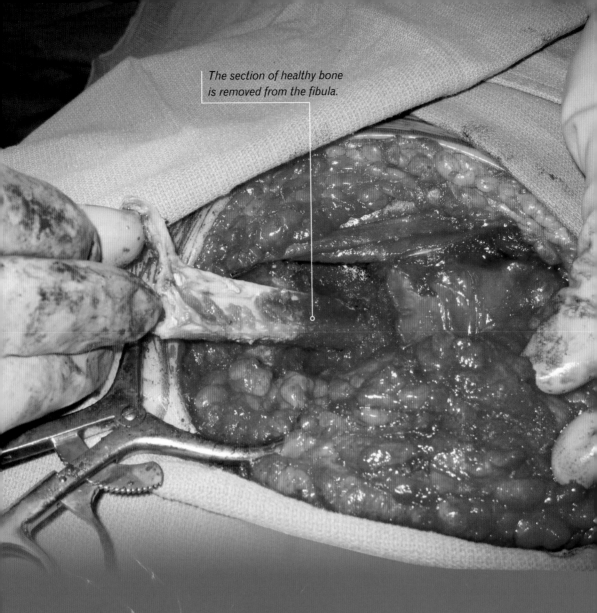

The section of healthy bone is removed from the fibula.

Jack's surgeon, Dr. James Urbaniak decided to repair Jack's hip joints with bone grafts. Bone grafts are pieces of healthy, living bone tissue. First, the medical team drilled out the unhealthy heads of Jack's femurs. Next, they removed a section of bone from Jack's fibula, the smaller of the two lower leg bones, to use as the graft.

Using tiny stitches, Dr. Urbaniak connected the graft's blood vessels to the femur's blood supply. That gave the grafted bone tissue the blood it needed to stay alive. Because it's living tissue, the bone graft produced new bone cells around itself. This way the transplant healed the same way a fracture does. The transplant became a permanent replacement for the dead bone.

Jack said, "I spent the better part of a year in a wheelchair. Then I had to be on crutches for months. I had to let my hip joints become strong enough to support my weight again. Finally, I worked out on a stationary bike to build up my strength."

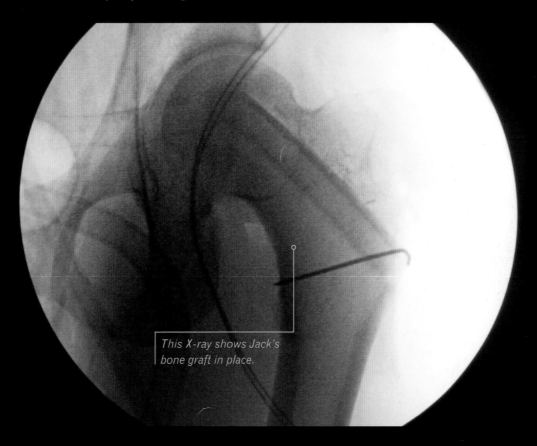

*This X-ray shows Jack's bone graft in place.*

SOMETIMES A SECTION OF BONE IS SHATTERED BEYOND REPAIR. A large piece may even poke through the skin and break off. For those cases, medical researchers have developed an artificial bone graft substitute. It can be used to fill the space where bone is missing. And it can be connected to the remaining living bone on either side of the fracture.

Wrists, ankles, and hips are the bones that most often break due to falls. A really hard fall can shatter a bone.

THE BONE GRAFT SUBSTITUTE IS SIMILAR TO A PROTEIN THE BODY MAKES TO HELP BONES HEAL. The protein has a spongelike structure, and the body's bone tissue cells collect on it. The protein structure helps support the newly forming bone tissue until it becomes strong and hard.

Once inserted, the bone graft substitute slowly starts to break down. The material contains calcium, which the new bone tissue absorbs.

# UPDATES

**BILKO WILLIAMS** is once again doing what he loves to do, performing daredevil stunts that thrill crowds.

**ALISHA CAPPS** is back pitching for her softball team. These days when she takes to the field, though, she wears a face mask. She's learned the value of protecting her bones. She has also started thinking about a career in medicine, helping people who suffer the kind of bone damage she survived.

ALISHA CAPPS

**JACK GRIFFETH** is a doctor treating cancer patients. In his spare time, he once again enjoys cycling, skiing, and mountain climbing.

Thanks to science and technological advances, doctors are able to restore bones once thought to be beyond repair. And people whose lives were shattered along with their bones are getting a second chance.

JACK GRIFFETH

## FOR YOUR BONES

Here are tips for living that will help your skeleton—and the rest of you—stay healthy.

- Exercise!  Walking, jogging, playing a sport, dancing—anything active helps bones stay strong.

- Drink milk.  Dairy products such as milk, cheese, and yogurt are sources of calcium.  So are broccoli, rice, and orange juice. Your bones need calcium to stay healthy. Drinking vitamin D-enriched milk is even better for your bones. Vitamin D helps bones absorb the calcium they need to stay strong.

- Wear the proper protective gear for sports and other activities, such as skateboarding.

- Reduce risks of falling at home. Keep floors free of toys and clutter. Get rid of throw rugs. Avoid standing on a chair to reach for things. Use a step stool instead.

- 

## BONES ARE AMAZING!

- Bones give your body its shape and protect your body's organs. They contain bone marrow, which produces the blood cells necessary for life.

- Within bones, cells are constantly destroying old bone tissue and building new.

- Bones make up only about one-fifth of the body's weight, but they support the entire body.

- The strongest bones in the body are the femurs—the leg bones that stretch from the hip to the knee.

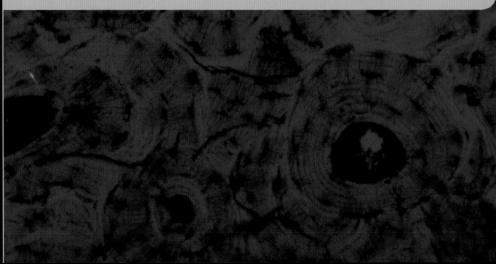

**bone graft:** a surgically replaced missing bone or a section that's been removed. This is done with bone material from the patient, another person, or with an artificial bone substitute.

**bone marrow:** the soft, spongy material found in the medullary cavities of bones. There are two types: yellow and red. Yellow is mainly fat. Red produces red blood cells, white blood cells, and platelets.

**calcium:** a mineral that makes bones hard

**collagen:** a strong, tough, fibrous material that is one of the building blocks of bones and cartilage

**compact bone:** a tightly packed bone tissue that forms the shaft of long bones and the outer part of other bones

**endosteum:** the thin membrane lining the medullary cavity

**fracture:** a break in a bone

**growth plate:** a disk at the end of a child's leg and arm bones that produces new bone tissue so that the bones can grow longer as the child ages

**ligaments:** stretchy bands that connect bones

**medullary cavity:** the central cavity of a bone shaft that contains bone marrow

**membrane:** a thin, flexible layer of tissue covering the outside of a body part or separating two connecting areas inside a body part

**osteoblast:** a cell that forms bone tissue

**osteoclast:** a cell that breaks down bone tissue and reabsorbs the minerals

**osteocyte:** a mature bone cell; what an osteoblast becomes after it is trapped within the tissue it helped form

**periosteum:** a membrane covering the surface of bones

**proteins:** substances that build body parts

**skeleton:** the body's strong, supportive framework made up of its many different bones

**spongy bone:** bony tissue with many open spaces or cavities that forms the ends of long bones and the inner part of other bones

**tendons:** stretchy bands that connect muscles to bones

**tissue:** a group of cells that have a similar structure and perform the same job for the body

**X-rays:** images made by passing high-energy X-rays through the body. These rays strike a photographic film or a computer plate. X-rays pass through soft tissue but are absorbed by solid tissue.

## MORE INFORMATION

**Want to learn more about your bones and the latest medical advancements for treating shattered bones? Check these resources.**

### BOOKS

Cobb, Vicki. *Your Body Battles a Broken Bone.* Minneapolis: Millbrook Press, 2009. Superhero cells work together to heal a broken bone in this illustrated book.

Johnson, Rebecca. *The Skeletal System.* Minneapolis: Lerner Publications Company, 2005. Text and pictures tell how bones work together in the human skeleton.

Parker, Steve. *Skeleton.* London: Dorling Kindersley, 2004. Investigate how muscles and bones work together and explore how bones change as they grow.

Walker, Richard. *The Human Skeleton.* London: Franklin Watts, 2007. Experiments in this book provide an opportunity for a hands-on investigation of the human skeleton.

### WEBSITES

BBC Science and Nature: The Interactive Body Skeleton
http://www.bbc.co.uk/science/humanbody/body/interactives/3djigsaw_02/index.shtml?skeleton
Leap into this site's exploration of bones and joints as you assemble a male or female skeleton. Follow the Fact File links to discover even more.

Kidport: Human Skeleton Overview Videos
http://www.kidport.com/RefLib/Science/HumanBody/SkeletalSystem/Video/SkeletonVideo.htm
There are a lot of fun activites on this site. Don't miss the Kid Science Stanley the Skeleton video.

How Stuff Works: How Do Broken Bones Heal?
http://health.howstuffworks.com/heal-broken-bones.htm
View video clips to understand bone structure and how broken bones heal themselves. Don't miss seeing how a man's bones saved him when he was swept into a tornado.

# SELECTED BIBLIOGRAPHY

## BOOKS

Lieberman, Jay R., and Gary E. Friedlaender, ed. *Bone Regeneration and Repair: Biology and Clinical Applications*. Totowa, NJ: Humana Press, 2005.

## NEWSPAPERS AND JOURNALS

Bartley, Nancy. "Doctor Rebuilds Faces—and Patient's Lives." *Seattle Times*, December 14, 2008. http:// seattletimes.nwsource.com/html/ localnews/2008513011_gruss14m.html (April 20, 2010).

Jones, Julian R., Eileen Gentleman, and Julia Polack. "Bioactive Glass Scaffolds for Bone Regeneration." *Elements* 3, no. 6 (December 2007): 393–399. Available online at http:// elements.geoscienceworld.org/cgi/ content/full/3/6/393 (May 25, 2009).

Nanowerk. "Nano-putty to Repair Serious Leg Fractures." *Nanowerk News*. January 26, 2009. http://www .nanowerk.com/news/newsid=9023. php (April 20, 2010).

"Nanotechnology Promises Bone Cell Regeneration." Nanotechnology Development Blog. March 31, 2007. http://www.nanotechnology development.com/medical/ nanotechnology-promises-bone-cell- regeneration.html (April 20, 2010).

*Science Daily*. "Synthetic Sea Worm Glue May Mend Shattered Knee, Face Bones." November 26, 2008. http://www.sciencedaily.com/ releases/2008/11/081125085620.htm (April 20, 2010).

## WEBSITES

BBC. "Broken Bones." BBC Science and Nature. n.d. http://www.bbc .co.uk/science/humanbody/body/ articles/skeleton/broken_bones .shtml (April 20, 2010).

University of Dayton. "Fixing What Ails Us." University of Dayton Research Institute. n.d. http://www.udri .udayton.edu/NR/exeres/6CCF7AF2- 8FE0-4037-96CD-BC7090797409.htm (May 25, 2009).

Inside Engineer. "New Bone Transplant Technology Is Under Development." n.d. http:// insideengineer.com/2008/12/new- bone-transplant-technology-is- under-development/#more-1263 (May 25, 2009).

## TELEPHONE INTERVIEWS

Capps, Alisha, February 12, 2009.

Capps, Leslie, February 12, 2009.

Ferrari, Mauro, February 25, 2009.

Griffeth, Jack, February 26, 2009.

Reiman, Paul, February 13, 2009.

Shuler, Franklin, February 12, 2009.

Stewart, Russell, February 3, 2009.

Stith, John, February 18, 2009.

Tarbet, Joyce, February 26, 2009.

Urbaniak, James, February 3, 2009.

Williams, Blake "Bilko," February 10, 2009.

# INDEX

# PHOTO CREDITS